ROCKS

Contents

What are rocks and minerals?

Rocks come in many different sizes, shapes, and colors, but they are all made up of pieces called minerals. What the rock is like depends on the minerals it contains. There are three main types: igneous, sedimentary, and metamorphic rocks.

Igneous rocks

Granite

Igneous rocks are usually hard.
They form when molten magma cools.

Sedimentary rocks

Sedimentary rocks form when layers of sand or mud are dried and crushed together. Gradually, they form a new layer of rock.

Sandstone

Metamorphic rocks

Metamorphic rocks form when existing rocks are heated and squeezed.

Marble

Minerals

Minerals are made up of different elements. Some minerals, such as gold, contain only one element but in most, two or more elements combine. If you look closely at some rocks, you can see the different minerals they contain.

Feldspar

Biotite

Quartz

5

Igneous rocks

Igneous rocks form when molten magma cools. The type of rock depends on the makeup of the magma and the speed of the cooling. Sometimes magma bursts out of volcanoes and cools quickly. But more often, it cools slowly, either deep within the Earth, or squeezed between existing rocks in the Earth's crust.

The magma pushes between other rocks.

The rocks here get very hot and squashed.

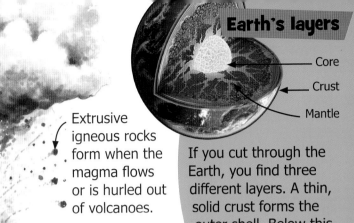

Earth's layers

Core

Crust

Mantle

Extrusive igneous rocks form when the magma flows or is hurled out of volcanoes.

If you cut through the Earth, you find three different layers. A thin, solid crust forms the outer shell. Below this, a thick layer of partly melted rock forms the mantle. In the middle is the metal core, part liquid and part solid.

Magma that flows out of a volcano is called lava. It cools quickly.

Intrusive igneous rocks form when magma cools under the surface of the Earth.

Red-hot magma builds up under the volcano.

Igneous rocks

Intrusive igneous rocks

Granite is made of quartz, feldspar, and mica.

Peridotite is heavy, with coarse grains.

Pegmatite has large crystals of feldspar, quartz, and mica.

In amygdaloidal basalt, minerals have formed in the air bubbles that were left as the basalt cooled

Dolerite is very common. It has medium-sized grains.

Serpentine is fine-grained. It contains quartz and feldspar.

Extrusive igneous rocks

Agglomerate is made up of rounded lumps of other igneous rocks.

Obsidian has a smooth surface. It splinters easily, forming sharp edges.

Pumice is full of gas bubbles and is very light. It will float on water.

Basalt is the most common lava rock. It forms when lava cools quickly and is fine-grained.

Rhyolite is fine-grained. It contains quartz and feldspar.

Tuff is formed from hardened volcanic ash.

Sedimentary rocks

Sedimentary rocks form from small pieces of rock, or sediment, together with the remains of animals and plants. Layers of sediment build up, are buried under other layers, and are squashed and cemented together.

Fossils

Fossils are the remains of things that lived in earlier times. Fossils are found mainly in sedimentary rocks.

The river wears away the floor of the valley and carries sediment towards the sea.

Layers of sediment build up on the seabed, mixed with the remains of sea animals.

Over millions of years, the layers are pressed togethe to form new rock.

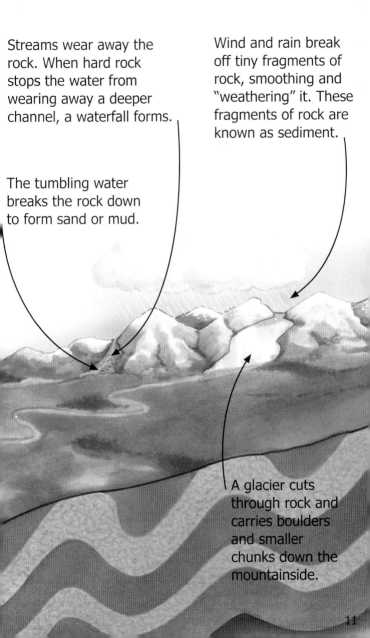

Streams wear away the rock. When hard rock stops the water from wearing away a deeper channel, a waterfall forms.

The tumbling water breaks the rock down to form sand or mud.

Wind and rain break off tiny fragments of rock, smoothing and "weathering" it. These fragments of rock are known as sediment.

A glacier cuts through rock and carries boulders and smaller chunks down the mountainside.

Clastic sedimentary rocks are made up of small pieces of other rocks.

Breccia is made up of angular pieces of other rock.

Mudstone is made up of hardened grains of mud.

Sandstone forms when grains of sand become cemented together.

Conglomerate contains rounded pebbles of other rock that have become cemented together.

Shale is similar to mudstone but breaks into thin sheets.

Clay has fine grains. It can be soft when wet.

Chemical sedimentary rocks form when an area of water evaporates and leaves behind salt and other minerals.

Biogenic sedimentary rocks are made up of shells and the other remains of living things.

Rock salt can be a range of different colors depending on the impurities it contains.

Limestone is made from calcite.

Stalactites form over thousands of years from the minerals in dripping water.

Chalk is a very pure, white limestone.

Flint is made of the mineral quartz. It is very hard.

Coal forms from squashed layers of plant material.

Metamorphic rocks

Metamorphic rocks are rocks that have been "changed." They form when igneous or sedimentary rocks are heated, crushed, or deeply buried. They are often harder than the original rock.

Volcanic heat

As lava forces its way through the Earth's crust, it heats and crushes the rocks nearby. The heat and the pressure change the whole makeup of the rock.

Tectonic plates

The Earth's crust is broken into sections called tectonic plates. These move very slowly, carried by the rock beneath them. When tectonic plates move towards each other, they squash layers of rock.

Meteorite crater

When meteorites hit the Earth, they melt or shatter the rock where they land.

Steatite is known as soapstone. It is soft and slippery to touch.

Eclogite is formed at very high temperatures deep in the Earth.

Marble forms when limestone is heated or squashed.

Gneiss has wavy bands of feldspar, mica, and quartz.

Quartzite forms when sandstone is heated or squashed.

Hornfels forms when mudstone or shale is heated.

Schist forms when mudstone and shale is heated and squashed.

Amphibolite is dark in color, with small flakes of black and white.

Migmatite is made of granite and gneiss.

Slate forms when mudstone or shale is heated or squashed.

Spotted slate splits into thin sheets. Its spots are all made of one mineral.

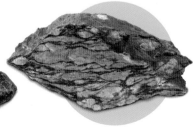

Mylonite is formed by stretching rock.

17

Rock minerals

Minerals are the building blocks that make up rocks. There are more than 4,000 different minerals. We can identify them in many ways, including their color, the way they break, how they reflect light, and how hard they are.

Nearly all minerals come in hard blocks called crystals.

Crystals have flat faces. Quartz crystals have six flat sides and end in a pyramid.

Most crystals have a regular shape.

Moh's scale

We can identify minerals by their hardness. Moh's scale of hardness grades minerals from 1 to 10. A mineral with a higher grade scratches those with a lower grade. Talc is the softest mineral and is 1, diamond is the hardest and is 10.

Purple
Amethyst
Quartz

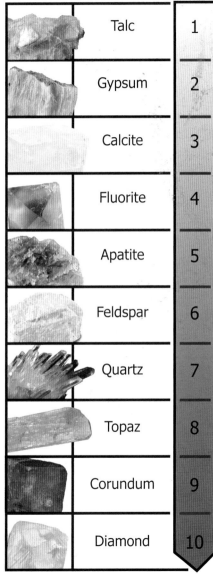

	Talc	1
	Gypsum	2
	Calcite	3
	Fluorite	4
	Apatite	5
	Feldspar	6
	Quartz	7
	Topaz	8
	Corundum	9
	Diamond	10

19

Gypsum forms when salty water evaporates. It is used to make a plaster when you break a leg.

Hornblende is commonly found in igneous and metamorphic rocks.

Garnet is a metamorphic mineral.

Olivine is usually a green color. It is not a common mineral.

Calcite is colorless or white.

Feldspar is found in igneous, metamorphic, and sedimentary rocks.

Quartz is very common. There are several different types of quartz.

Mica is a mineral that glitters. Light is reflected from its flat surfaces.

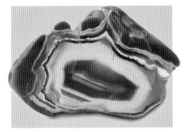

Augite is mainly found in igneous rocks.

Agate has very fine grains. It is often a bright color.

Staurolite is a reddish-brown color.

Kyanite is a deep blue color. It has long, column-shaped crystals.

Gemstones

Gemstones are crystals that are especially beautiful and valuable. People cut and polish them to improve their color or shine and often set them in jewelry.

Rough diamonds look like pebbles of cloudy glass.

Hard diamonds

Diamonds are made of pure carbon and are very hard. The lead in your pencil is also made of pure carbon, but it is called graphite and is soft. Diamonds form in igneous rocks when there is great heat and pressure. They are rare and valuable.

When a diamond is cut and polished, it sparkles and shines.

Diamond set in a ring

Diamonds are the hardest natural material. So only a diamond can cut another diamond.

Blue or green?

Emeralds and aquamarines form from the same mineral, called beryl. The contrasting colors result from different impurities.

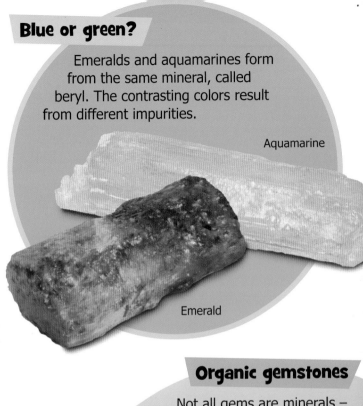

Aquamarine

Emerald

Organic gemstones

Not all gems are minerals – some come from plants and animals. For example, pearls form inside oyster shells.

23

Birthstones

January

Garnet

February

Amethyst

March

Aquamarine

July

Ruby

August

Peridot

September

Sapphire

24

Gemstones have been chosen for each month of the year. Your birthstone is the gemstone for the month in which you were born.

Diamond

Emerald

Pearl

Opal

Citrine

Turquoise

Ore minerals

Ores are minerals that contain metals. People can remove the metal by heating the ores or using electricity.

Chalcopyrite is the most common ore for copper. Copper is also found on its own, not in an ore.

Iron is the metal that we use most of all.

Hematite is the main ore that contains iron. It is often red in color.

Ore: Hematite
Metal: Iron

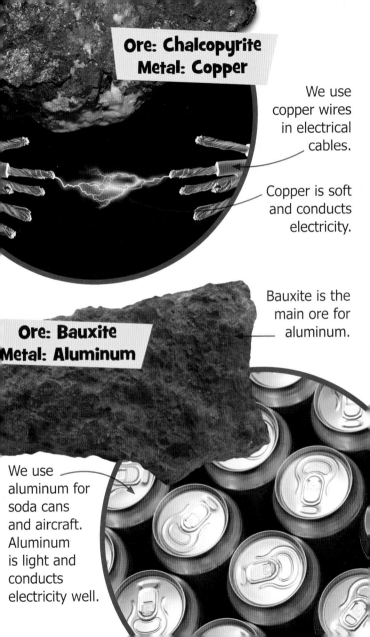

Ore: Chalcopyrite
Metal: Copper

We use copper wires in electrical cables.

Copper is soft and conducts electricity.

Bauxite is the main ore for aluminum.

Ore: Bauxite
Metal: Aluminum

We use aluminum for soda cans and aircraft. Aluminum is light and conducts electricity well.

Ore minerals

Gold does not usually mix with the rock it is in.

Silver is silver-white when it is found, but turns a dull black color in the air.

Rutile is a red color. It contains titanium, a strong but very light metal.

Sphalerite is the main ore of zinc. It is usually a brown-black color.

Galena contains lead and sulphur. It is found in sedimentary rocks.

Magnetite is a strong natural magnet. Its crystals are small and black.

Copper is found in a range of different ores.

Malachite is a common copper ore. It is bright green.

Bornite is nicknamed peacock ore because of its coloring.

Azurite is a deep blue color. It is used to make dyes for paints and cloth.

Wolframite is black or red-brown. It contains iron, manganese, and tungsten.

Rhodochrosite is a very attractive bright pink-rose color.

Pyrolusite contains manganese, which we need to make steel. It is a dull black color.

Glossary

This glossary explains some of the harder words in the book.

biogenic
Sedimentary rock formed from the remains of living things.

chemical
Sedimentary rock formed when water evaporates, leaving minerals behind.

clastic Sedimentary rock formed from small pieces of other rock.

core Found at the very center of the Earth, the core is partly made of liquid metal.

extrusive Igneous rock that has cooled at the Earth's surface.

fossil The remains of something that lived in an earlier age.

gemstone
A mineral that looks very beautiful when cut and polished.

glacier A very large section of ice that moves slowly downhill.

igneous Rock formed when molten magma cools.

intrusive Igneous rock that has cooled slowly inside the Earth's crust.

magma Molten rock from inside the Earth.

mantle A very large layer of solid rock underneath the Earth's crust.

metamorphic Rock formed by heating or crushing existing rock.

meteorite The remains of an object that has come from outer space and struck the Earth.

minerals The elements that make up rocks.

ore minerals
Minerals that contain metals.

sedimentary Rock formed when layers of sand or mud are dried and crushed.

tectonic plates The large sections into which the Earth's crust is broken.